Ready to Learn
Verbs

How To Play

1 Press the Power button to turn the SD-X Reader on or off. The LED will light up when the SD-X Reader is on.

2 Touch the volume buttons found on this page to adjust the volume.

3 Touch words and pictures on the page to hear audio. These icons start the following activities:

 Hear the sentence.

 Hear the word.

 Spell the word.

4 After two minutes of inactivity, the SD-X Reader will beep and go to sleep.

5 If the batteries are low, the SD-X Reader will beep twice and the LED will start blinking. Replace the batteries by following the instructions on the preceding page. The SD-X Reader uses two AAA batteries.

6 To use headphones or earbuds, plug them into the headphone jack on the SD-X Reader.

Volume

Publications International, Ltd.

SD·X
INTERACTIVE

The Letter A

Add If you **add** all the balloons together you get ten.

Agree The cat and dog **agree**.

Arrive The turtle **arrives** on the train.

Ask The badger **asks** the turtle when the train is leaving.

The Letter B

Bake I will **bake** a cake today.

Be I have to **be** in the city by noon.

Bite The alligator **bites** the apple.

Bounce Monkey **bounces** on his suitcase.

Break I did not mean to **break** the window.

Bring The bear **brings** a picnic lunch.

Build I wonder what the ducks will **build**.

Buy The gorilla wants to **buy** some fruit.

Monkey Town Station

This place is bananas!

The Letter

Call The captain **calls** the players onto the field.

Carry The dog **carries** the shirt away.

Catch The zebra will flip the quarter and **catch** it.

Chase The purple elephant is too slow to **chase** dogs!

Cheer We **cheer** when our team scores.

Choose **Choose** a ball from the pile.

Clean It is hard to **clean** such a big mess.

Climb Monkey **climbs** up onto the goalpost.

Close The hippo can't **close** his mouth.

Come They **come** to games early.

Count **Count** the number of clouds you see.

Crawl The pig **crawls** over the line.

Let's go, Pineapples!

The Big Game

The Letter D

Decide Pineapple or grapes—the raccoon can't **decide**!

Draw Monkey **draws** a funny face on the banana.

Dress The rabbit **dresses** for work.

Drink Camels **drink** lots of water.

Drive The buffalo **drives** to the store for a snack.

Drop If you **drop** something, pick it up!

Dry That walrus should **dry** himself off.

The Letter E

Eat Penguins love to **eat** snow cones.

Enjoy The polar bears **enjoy** shopping here.

Enter Let's **enter** the store and find a cart.

Exit The alligator **exits** through the door.

"Buy a Bunch" Grocery Store

Cleanup on aisle everywhere!

The Letter F

Fall I hope Monkey does not **fall**!

Feed The farmer **feeds** the cow.

Feel The two goats **feel** happy today.

Fill The farmer **fills** the bin with corn.

Find The pig **finds** a shiny penny.

Finish The dog will **finish** bringing the sheep home.

Float A frog **floats** on the log.

Follow The ducklings **follow** their mother.

The Letter

Give She **gives** him a sandwich.

Glow The windows **glow**.

Go He will **go** to the field on his tractor.

Grow Corn **grows** in the summer.

Guess **Guess** how many chickens got out.

Papa Pig's Family Farm

They're hogging all the fun!

The Letter H

Hang Monkey **hangs** by his tail.

Have These bears **have** blue fur!

Hear He **hears** someone yelling.

Help "**Help** me, I am stuck!" yells the big bear.

Hide The little bear **hides** in back of the truck.

Hold A truck can **hold** a lot of bags.

This pla is fur re

The Letter I

Imagine She can **imagine** having her own skates.

Invite **Invite** your friends to come inside.

The Letter J

Join She runs to **join** her friends.

Juggle He **juggles** three pots.

Jump The baby bear likes to **jump** up and down.

The Letter K

Keep She will **keep** both of the pots.

Kick The bear **kicks** the can.

Bear City

The Letter

Kiss The skunk **kisses** the dog.

Knock He **knocks** on the box.

Know Monkey **knows** what time it is.

The Letter

Laugh Monkey makes her **laugh**.

Leap Look at that frog **leap**.

Learn The penguin **learns** how to fly.

Lick He **licks** the lollipop.

Lift This suitcase is hard to **lift**.

Like The lion **likes** to fly.

Listen He **listens** to music.

Look The owl **looks** out the window at the airplane.

Love The bunnies **love** each other.

Monkey Town Airport

Orange you glad you flew Banana?

The Letter M

Make He likes to **make** toy airplanes.

Meet Two hamsters **meet** each other.

Melt The ice cream **melts** on the floor.

Miss She **misses** her ice cream.

The Letter N

Nap She likes to **nap** under the window.

Nod The giraffe **nods**.

Notice The turtle **notices** the monkey in the tree.

Obey He **obeys** the teacher.

Offer He **offers** his ice cream to her.

Open The little pig **opens** the door.

The Letter P

Paint She **paints** a monkey.

Pay The calf will **pay** for the carton of milk.

Pick The hamster **picks** his favorite toy.

My best subject is snack time!

Miss Moose's Schoolroom

Plant Let's **plant** a tree.

Play She **plays** with her toys.

Pour She **pours** the water out of the bowl.

Pull It is time to **pull** down the lights.

Push Monkey **pushes** his friend.

Put Now the bear can **put** the shovel down.

The Letter Q

Quit The turtle **quits** running.

Reach The blue bunny **reaches** for the baseball.

Read The owl **reads** a book.

Receive He **receives** a box.

Rest It is nice to **rest** under a tree.

Ride The pig **rides** his bike around the block.

Run The leopard **runs** past the turtle.

Monkey's Neighborhood

The Letter S

Sail The boat **sails** across the pond.

Save He **saves** his money for later.

See Monkey **sees** what everyone is doing.

Sell He **sells** fresh coconuts.

Shake The elephant **shakes** the tree.

Share He **shares** his bananas with Monkey.

Sing The warthog likes to **sing** when he is happy.

Sit The other monkey **sits** in the tree.

Sleep Now he **sleeps** in the sun.

Smell The alligator does not like what he **smells**!

Spill She **spills** her juice.

I'm always "hanging around"!

Jungle Fun

The Letter

Start The alligator will **start** cleaning the floor.

Stop "**Stop** throwing bread!" says the pig.

Subtract **Subtract** one from five to get four.

Swim A bug is **swimming** in my soup!

The Letter

Talk Monkey loves to **talk**.

Taste This soup **tastes** funny.

Thank He **thanks** the waiter.

Think The hippo **thinks** he will make pizza.

Throw He **throws** a piece of bread.

Toss She **tosses** it in her mouth.

Touch An elephant can **touch** with his trunk.

Travel The bus **travels** down the road.

Where you can really eat like an animal!

"Feeding Time" Diner

The Letter

Use Use the ladder to climb up high.

The Letter

View He **views** a picture of his grandpa.

Visit The class **visits** the museum.

The Letter

Wait Wait behind the red rope.

Wake The guard **wakes** up.

Walk The rhino **walks** through the museum.

Want The llama really **wants** the toy.

Wash I will **wash** this side first.

Watch The giraffe **watches** everything closely.

Wave Monkey **waves** to everybody.

Wear No one knows why he **wears** that hat.

Win She hopes her ticket **wins** the prize!

It's older than a brown banana!

Museum of Really Old Stuff

The Letter W

Wish The rhino **wishes** it was his turn on the slide.

Write She **writes** her ideas in a book.

The Letter Y

Yawn He **yawns** because he is tired.

Yell He **yells** to his friends.

The Letter Z

Zoom Monkey **zooms** down the slide!

Let's monkey around again some time!

The Big Slide